Harley,
The
Throwaway Puppy

Written and Illustrated
by
Elisabeth Davis

Grizzlie Books
www.grizzliebooks.com

For my family and our dogs.

Other books by Elisabeth Davis:
Mo: A Throwaway Puppy Story (2012)
Brae Visits Arran (U.K. version), printed in Scotland (2011)
Brae and the Mystery of Arran (U.S. version, 2011)

This is Harley.

She doesn't know it yet, but
she is a champion. She just
needs one thing now.

A family.

The little puppy sat still in her cage. All around her, new noises filled her ears and new smells tickled her moist black nose.

Why was she here?

Strange people gave her food, and other strangers came to look into her kennel.

"Is this my home?" she wondered.

Her soft, light-brown puppy fur and silly ears -- one up and one down -- did not look like the other dogs around her.

Her puppy eyes became sad as she sat still and waited and waited.

Someone had thrown her away.

Not very far away from the puppy, two young people lived on a farm filled with horses, a little donkey, two cats, and lots of love.

After a while, the couple saw that the farm was the perfect place for a dog.

So, they began to search for a puppy who needed a home, a puppy who wasn't like all the others.

One day, they saw a photo of a sad-eyed puppy with silly ears -- one up and one down.

The puppy had been up for adoption for weeks and weeks.

But no one had come for her.

The young couple drove to the adoption center, hoping to find the sad-eyed puppy in the photo.

There she was!

Her silly ears -- one up and one down -- perked as she heard their voices coming to her cage. Instead of walking on by, they stopped.

Hello, puppy," they called softly. "Don't be scared. Do you want to come home?"

The little puppy listened carefully, but she was still afraid.

More strangers, she sighed to herself.

But these strangers seemed very kind and gentle.

They loaded her in their car, drove to their farm, gave her a warm bed and some toys and treats, and talked to her.

"What shall we call you, silly puppy? Harley? Do you like the name Harley?"

This new family played games with her and gave her cuddles and hugs. They taught the puppy how to sit and stay. She was such a quick learner!

Each day, Harley raced like the wind around the pastures, until, finally, one day the sadness left her eyes, replaced by joy.

The little puppy with the silly ears -- one up and one down -- was finally home.

As she grew, her puppy legs became strong and tall, just right for jumping and zigzagging.

The young couple soon realized that Harley needed more than just running around the farm. Going to school was just the thing for a growing pup who could jump so high and run so fast.

They all enrolled in an agility class.

In agility, dogs learn how to leap over jumps, race through tunnels, weave through lines of poles, and lots of other exciting activities.

Harley was a quick learner.

At first, she was a little afraid of all the new things she had to do.

However, in no time, she was running around the agility course, jumping and weaving, and having fun.

Good girl, Harley.

One day, the young couple got Harley ready to go on a trip with them.

They told her that she would be in an agility competition, a test of how well she could listen to them.

Harley was ready.

On the day of the competition, Harley was a little bit nervous.

Dogs raced around the course in front of them -- up and down, in and out, over and through.

They made it look so easy, but Harley knew all the dogs were paying close attention to their families.

Finally, it was Harley's turn. The young couple told her she was wonderful and that she should just have fun.

Ready, set, go!

Harley began by leaping over five small jumps. She raced up the bridge and over the top.

Harley darted through the tunnel.

The weave poles were next, and Harley dashed back and forth, listening carefully to her family about what came next. She was having so much fun!

The course was over in a flash.

Harley leapt into her family's arms, licking their faces with happiness.

They hugged and petted her and told her she was the best dog in the world.

Then came the biggest surprise of all.

Harley had won a ribbon!

Her family was so proud of her.

She had started life as a throwaway puppy, a dog no one wanted.

And now Harley was a champion.

You see, all she needed was a family to love her.

But the best secret was that in her family's eyes, Harley had always been a champion.

The dog with the silly ears -- one up and one down -- had won their hearts.

In the years since Harley's first agility trial, this boxer-German Shepherd mixed-breed dog has gone on to win many ribbons and titles with her family, James and Kristen.

With each competition, Harley proves to everyone that all dogs can be champions --
if someone loves them.

Harley's Titles:
USDAA: APD PJM APS APK APG APR
AKC: MX MXJ OF (working on her MACH title)
Splash Dogs: Senior Dog, Gold Medal
In 2012, Harley was one of just 29 mixed-breed dogs to qualify for the AKC National Agility Championships.

Author and illustrator Elisabeth Davis is a former college English professor who began to dabble in watercolors while still teaching. Her gentle and hopeful books combine her love of children, story telling, painting, and animals. The true stories of her son and daughter-in-law's shelter dogs Harley and Mo inspired her to create children's books about these wonderful agility champions. **All proceeds are donated to animal rescue charities.**

Davis' first book -- <u>Harley, The Throwaway Puppy</u> -- has raised hundreds of dollars for animal rescue charities. For more information, visit her website at <u>www.grizzliebooks.com</u>. Facebook fans can join her at <u>www.facebook.com/HarleyThrowawayPuppy</u>.

Please donate to an animal rescue charity of your choice, and if you can, share your life with an adopted pet.

Published by Grizzlie Books

For more information on this book and other products,
go to
www.grizzliebooks.com

Made in the USA
Charleston, SC
06 September 2015